Ingrid Preedy

Ben Alone in Leeds

Ernst Klett Verlag
Stuttgart Düsseldorf Leipzig

Zu dieser Lektüre gibt es eine Kassette (Klettnummer 570921)

Gedruckt auf Recyclingpapier, hergestellt aus 100 % Altpapier.

1. Auflage A 1 8 7 | 2006 05 04

Alle Drucke dieser Auflage können im Unterricht nebeneinander benutzt werden. Die letzte Zahl bezeichnet das Jahr dieses Druckes.

Internetadresse: http://www.klett.de

Zeichnungen: Peter Gray, London.
Druck: Wilhelm Röck, Weinsberg
Printed in Germany.

ISBN 3-12-570920-2

Contents

Chapter 1: It's Saturday morning

"It's breakfast time," says Mrs Batts. Ben opens one eye and looks at his mother.

"Come on, it's time to get up," his mother says.

"Must I go to kindergarten today? Can't I stay at home and play in the garden?" he asks.

"Yes, you can. You're not going to kindergarten today."

"Is it not open today?" asks Ben.

"No, it isn't open because today is Saturday. The kindergarten is never open on Saturday," says Mrs Batts and laughs.

Ben jumps out of bed and runs downstairs to the kitchen.

Yes, it's Saturday morning. And it's always the same on Saturday mornings – Mr Batts gets up at 8 o'clock and makes the breakfast. He makes bacon and eggs for Mrs Batts and Carol, and he makes toast, a lot of toast, for Ben. Then he wakes Mrs Batts. She then wakes Carol and Ben. They all have breakfast in the kitchen, and then Mr and Mrs Batts go into Leeds. They always go shopping at the supermarket and then at the market. They sometimes have a cup of coffee in a little snack bar in Mushroom Street, and then they go home.

1	**eye** [aɪ]	Auge
5	**ask** [ɑ:sk]	fragen
10	**laugh** [lɑ:f]	lachen
17	**wake** [weɪk]	wecken

"Can you buy some jam today, please?" asks Ben at the breakfast table. "Look, there is no jam."

"Ben! I'm always buying jam for you! Do you eat jam without toast? OK, jam from the supermarket for Ben," says Mrs Batts.

"And can you buy some apples, please? I always go to the swimming pool with Linda on Sundays, and we're always hungry when we swim," says Carol.

"Yes, dear, we can buy apples at the market. They've got good apples there," answers her mother.

Now Carol and Ben are alone in the kitchen. Their mother and father are in Leeds. Carol is washing the dishes. She always washes the dishes and cleans the kitchen on Saturdays. Ben sometimes helps her. Today he's helping her. He's drying the dishes. But Carol isn't very happy about it.

"Look, Ben. You can dry the dishes, but don't break them. Don't dry the knives. They can hurt you. They're dangerous for a little boy."

Ben dries the dishes, but he doesn't dry the knives.

"Oh, the phone!" says Carol. It's Linda, and Carol talks to her. Carol and Linda always talk for a long time.

"What can I dry now?" thinks Ben. He takes a cup. "I can dry this cup," he thinks.

4	**without** [wɪð'aʊt]	ohne
11	**alone** [ə'ləʊn]	allein
16	**break** [breɪk]	kaputtmachen, (zer)brechen
17	**knife, knives** [naɪf, naɪvs]	Messer
17	**hurt** [hɜːt]	verletzen

"Wait a minute, Linda," says Carol to her friend, "Ben is drying a cup. That's not a good idea."

"Don't worry, he's a big boy. He can dry a cup," says Linda on the phone.

But then the cup falls and breaks.

"Oh, Ben! That is Mum's cup. She always drinks out of that cup. You're a very silly boy!" Carol is very angry. "Go to your room. You can break things there."

Ben goes to his room.

Carol talks to Linda again.

1 **a minute** ['mɪnɪt] eine Minute; *hier:* ein Augenblick
7 **silly** ['sɪlɪ] dumm, blöde
7 **angry** ['æŋgrɪ] böse, zornig

"The cup?" asks Linda.

"Yes, the cup – Mum's favourite cup. I say, '*You can dry the dishes but don't break them*'. Then I talk to you for two minutes, and what does he do? He dries Mum's cup, her favourite cup. And then the cup falls and it breaks! Silly boy! Little brothers are a big problem."

The two girls talk for twenty minutes. They go to the same school, they are in the same class and they meet every day. Their parents can't understand why they talk on the phone for hours.

"What do you talk about?" Linda's father asks.

"Things," answers Linda.

"School starts in thirty minutes. Why are you talking to Linda on the phone now?" Carol's mother often asks.

"There's not enough time at school," says Carol.

Ben's in his bedroom now and he's sad. He sits on his bed. Then he takes his toy dog and talks to it. That helps a little. Then he looks around his room at his things. In a corner he sees his piggy bank. He has an idea. He goes back to the kitchen.

"Carol," he says.

"Yes?" says Carol.

"I'm sorry. But I've got an idea. Look, here's my piggy bank. I can buy Mum a new cup," says Ben.

2	**favourite** ['feɪvrɪt]	Lieblings-
9	**parents** ['peərənts]	Eltern
15	**enough** [ɪ'nʌf]	genug
16	**sad** [sæd]	traurig
17	**a little** ['lɪtl]	ein bisschen
19	**piggy bank** [pɪgɪ bæŋk]	Sparschwein

Carol looks at Ben and thinks, "He's a nice little brother. And that's a nice idea. But he can't go into Leeds alone. I want to meet Linda in town at two o'clock – I can take him with me."

Carol looks at Ben. "How much money have you got in your piggy bank?" she asks.

"One hundred pounds."

"No, Ben, I don't think so – not a hundred pounds. Give me the key and we can open your piggy bank and see."

The children open the piggy bank. There is not one hundred pounds. There is not ten pounds. There is only two pounds twenty.

"Can I buy a cup with that?" asks Ben.

"Yes, I think so," answers Carol.

3	**I want to meet**	ich will treffen
12	**only** ['əʊnlɪ]	nur

Chapter 2: In town

Carol and Ben sit upstairs on the bus to Leeds, and Ben looks at everything in the street.

"Look, Carol, there's a pet shop. I can see little dogs in the window. Carol, can I have a dog for my birthday?"

"No, Ben, you can't. Mum always says, '*No dogs*.' Look, there's my friend Kevin in the snack bar over there."

"Kevin! Kevin!" shouts Ben.

"Ben, don't shout. He can't hear you."

"Oh, yes, OK. Look! Over there, next to the bank! A policeman. And he's talking to that man. Is that a robber? Yes, I think he's a robber. He's got a big, black bag. And there's a lot of money in it."

"No, Ben! That's my English teacher and that's not a bag of money. That's his school bag with our English tests in it! He always goes to his mother's house on Saturdays, and he always takes our English tests with him!"

Ten minutes later Carol is in the street with Ben. They are opposite Kirkgate Market. Carol takes Ben's hand and they go into the market.

"Oh wow! It's a big market! You can buy a lot of things here," says Ben. "Look, over there! There's a stall with toys. Carol, let's look at them!"

2	**everything** ['evrɪθɪŋ]	alles
7	**shout** [ʃaʊt]	(laut) rufen, schreien
16	**test** [test]	Test, Klassenarbeit
17	**late, later** [leɪt, 'leɪtə]	spät, später
21	**stall** [stɔ:l]	(Markt)Stand

"No, not now. I want to meet Linda at Manny's fish stall. Manny's got the best fish in Leeds and Linda buys fish for her mother there every Saturday. And then we can look at the toys," says Carol. She goes to Manny's fish stall with Ben, but Linda is not there.

"Where is Linda?" asks Ben.

"It's not two o'clock. We must wait ten minutes. We always meet here at two o'clock. You can look at the fish."

Ben looks at the fish. There are big fish and small fish, red fish and white fish. Ben doesn't like fish.

"Fish are boring," he thinks. Suddenly he sees another toy stall with a big red bus on it. There are a lot of people in the market, and Ben isn't a big boy. He can't see all the toys. Ben looks at Carol and then at the toy stall. Carol is talking to the man behind the fish stall.

"I can see the toy stall from here and I can see Carol from here. Then I can see Carol from the the toy stall, too," Ben thinks.

Ben goes to the toy stall and looks at all the toys. There are so many different things there.

"I can't have a real dog for my birthday, but perhaps I can have a toy dog or a teddy bear or a computer. I don't know what a computer is, but my friend Mark in kindergarten always says, '*Computers are great!*' He plays with his computer every day," thinks Ben. "Oh, there's a big toy dog over there and a cowboy hat and a football. What is best? It's so difficult. Why can't I have a birthday every day?"

1 **fish** [fɪʃ] — Fisch
21 **real** [riːəl] — echt, wirklich
21 **perhaps** [pə'hæps] — vielleicht
22 **teddy bear** ['tedɪ beə] — Teddy(bär)
26 **hat** [hæt] — Hut

Ben forgets Carol. Ten minutes later he suddenly remembers her and the fish stall, but when he goes back to the fish stall Carol is not there. He looks at all the stalls next to the fish stall, but he can't see Carol.

"What now?" he thinks. "Oh, yes, I remember: Linda wants to buy the new 'Monsters of Rock' CD. I can look at the stalls with CDs and then I can find Linda and Carol."

Ben looks for Carol and Linda. He sees stalls with jeans and T-shirts, stalls with books and stalls with apples and bananas. But he can't see a stall with CDs. He looks at a lot of stalls. There are a lot of people in the market. Some are buying things and some are only looking. But for a little boy a lot of people mean a lot of legs. Sometimes Ben has a problem with all the legs. He can't always see what is on the stalls. Where are the CDs? Where is Carol? He can only see legs.

13 **mean** [mi:n] bedeuten
13 **leg** [leg] Bein

Chapter 3: Anne

Soon Ben is very tired and hungry. He sees a stall with nice, red apples.

"How much are those red apples, please?" he asks the woman behind the stall.

"The red apples cost £1.50 a pound," she says.

"And how much are those green apples?"

"They're £1.75 a pound," answers the woman.

"I only want one apple," says Ben.

"Let's see. This red apple is 20p and this green one is 35p."

"Oh, good. I like green apples. Oh, no! Wait a minute. I haven't got 35p. My sister Carol has got my money."

"And where is your sister?"

"I don't know."

"Well, no money – no apples. Sorry! Now go away. I've got a lot of work today."

Ben walks away.

"She's not a very nice woman," he thinks. He sits down between a cheese stall and a bread stall. Now he's very hungry. He looks at the bread; then he looks at the cheese.

"No money – no bread and cheese!" he thinks.

"Hello, what's your name?"

1	**soon** [su:n]	bald
1	**tired** ['taɪəd]	müde
19	**between** [bɪ'twi:n]	zwischen
19	**cheese** [tʃi:z]	Käse
19	**bread** [bred]	Brot

Ben looks around. A little girl is watching him. She sits down next to him. She's got brown hair and very big brown eyes.

"Me? Eh ... My name's Ben. What's your name?"

"My name's Anne. Are you here alone? Where are your parents?"

"They're at home. I'm here with my sister Carol."

"And where is she?"

"I don't know." Ben tells Anne his story. "And now I'm very hungry and tired," he says.

"That's no problem," says Anne. "There's a cheese stall and there's a bread stall."

"But Carol's got my money. I have no money. No money – no bread and cheese!" says Ben.

"Wait here," says Anne.

She goes to the bread stall and takes two white rolls. Then she goes to the cheese stall. There she takes cheese for the rolls. Ben watches her. His mouth is open. Anne doesn't pay. She doesn't pay the woman at the bread stall and she doesn't pay the man at the cheese stall.

"You can't do that. I'm not eating those rolls or that cheese. You must pay for things. My mother always pays for things. That's not good. No, no. Now look! That man's talking on the phone. Is he talking to the police? What can we do? Can we run away or is there no time?" Ben is very worried.

2	**hair** [heə]	Haar(e)
9	**tell**	erzählen, sagen
16	**roll** [rəʊl]	Brötchen
18	**mouth** [maʊθ]	Mund
19	**pay** [peɪ]	bezahlen
26	**worried** ['wʌrɪd]	besorgt, beunruhigt

"Hey, don't worry! The woman behind the bread stall is my mother and the man at the cheese stall is my father. He isn't talking to the police. He's talking to a man at another cheese stall because he wants some goat's cheese."

"Oh, I see. They're your parents."

"Yes, I always come with them on Saturdays. I meet a lot of nice people here. I know all the people behind the stalls. Some of them are nice and some of them are not. Over there is Mr White with his pet stall," says Anne.

"Oh, yes, pets. Let's go and look. Is he nice – Mr White?" asks Ben.

"Yes, he's very nice. But wait a minute," answers Anne. She goes back to her mother and then she comes back with a big bag.

"I've got a bag with old bread. We can give it to Mr White for his guinea pigs," she says.

"I want a dog for my birthday, but my Mum says, '*No dogs*'," says Ben.

The two children go to Mr White's pet stall and look at the pets. They play with the little cats and the baby guinea pigs.

"This little brown rabbit is nice," says Ben. "Can I pick him up?" he asks.

"Yes, but be careful," says Mr White.

Ben picks up the little brown rabbit. It looks at him with its little black eyes and then it bites his little finger.

4 **goat** [gəʊt]	Ziege
14 **bag**	*hier:* Tüte
22 **pick up** [pɪk ʌp]	aufheben, hochheben
24 **be careful** [bi: ˈkeəfʊl]	sei vorsichtig, pass' auf!
26 **bite** [baɪt]	beißen
26 **finger** [ˈfɪŋgə]	Finger

"Oww!" he shouts and drops the rabbit. The little rabbit runs under the stall.

"Oh no! Ben! The rabbit! It's under the stall. You must find it," says Anne.

"Not me. That rabbit bites. I'm not going under the stall for it. You can go. It's dangerous," says Ben. He looks at his finger.

"Silly! It's a little rabbit and you're a big boy. And you've got all your fingers."

"But it hurts," says Ben.

Anne goes under the stall for the rabbit, but the rabbit doesn't want to come back. It runs away. It sees a stall with green things on it. It starts to eat them.

1 **drop** [drɒp] fallen lassen
13 **start to eat** anfangen zu essen

"Hey! Those are my lettuces. That rabbit is eating my lettuces! Whose rabbit is it? I want money for those lettuces. I can't sell them now," shouts a very big man with a very red face.

Anne catches the rabbit and runs. Ben wants to talk to the man and tell him about the rabbit and his little finger. But he looks at the man and the man looks at him, and then Ben runs. He follows Anne. He can see her because she is wearing a red T-shirt. She runs back to Mr White and gives him the rabbit. Then she takes Ben's hand and runs between the stalls. Ben doesn't know where they are, but he's not worried. He's with Anne, and that big man with the red face is not behind them.

"That's Mr Dancer, but I think his name's Mr Dangerous. I think he eats children," says Anne.

Now Ben *is* worried!

"I think it's time to go home now," says Ben to Anne.

"Can you come again and play with me again? I'm always here on Saturdays."

"Yes, OK. But I must ask my Mum. Bye."

"Bye," says Anne.

1 **lettuce** ['letɪs] Kopfsalat
3 **sell** [sel] verkaufen
4 **face** [feɪs] Gesicht
5 **catch** [kætʃ] fangen

Chapter 4: On the bus

"I don't know where Carol is. Perhaps she's at home now. Perhaps she's at Linda's house, or perhaps she's in a CD shop. But I can't find her. I want to go home. I don't want to stay here alone," thinks Ben.

He walks out of the market and along the road. Then he sees a bus stop. There is a woman with four children, two boys and two girls there. A bus comes.

"Here's the thirty-three. That's our bus," says the woman to her children.

"I must take a three, too," thinks Ben and gets on with the family. Oh dear! Ben is not very good with numbers!

The woman buys a family ticket and the bus driver says: "One, two, three, four, five children. You've got a very big family!"

But the woman doesn't hear him. She goes upstairs with the children. Ben goes upstairs, too. He sits next to an old man with a dog. He can see everything in the street. He can see big shops and a lot of houses. The bus stops at all the bus stops and people get on and off.

"What's your dog's name?" Ben asks the old man next to him.

"Rover."

6	**bus stop** ['bʌs stɒp]	Bushaltestelle
10	**get on**	einsteigen
11	**oh, dear!** [əʊ 'dɪə]	meine Güte!
12	**ticket** ['tɪkɪt]	Fahrkarte
12	**driver** ['draɪvə]	Fahrer
19	**get off**	aussteigen

"Does he bite?"

"Only little boys – because they always ask silly questions," says the man.

Ben is worried, but the man laughs. Then Ben laughs, too.

"I want a dog for my birthday but my Mum says, '*No dogs*'," says Ben.

"A dog is a lot of work," says the old man. "You can't put it in a cupboard when you have no time. You must always play with it and take it for a walk every day."

"That's OK. I can take it for a walk every day. I only go to kindergarten in the morning," says Ben.

"And in winter?"

"In winter I can play with the dog in my room," answers Ben.

"No, you must take a dog for a walk every day in winter, too," says the old man.

"That's OK. My sister can take it for a walk in winter. I can't play outside in winter. But Carol always goes to her friend Linda's house in summer and in winter. She can take the dog with her then," says Ben.

The man wants to give Ben a piece of chocolate. Ben looks at the chocolate. He likes chocolate and he's hungry.

"No, thank you," he says to the man. "My mother always says, '*Don't take chocolate from strange people.*' " He looks at the chocolate. "That's very good chocolate. It's my favourite chocolate," he says.

3	**question** ['kwestʃən]	Frage
22	**a piece** [pi:s] **of chocolate**	ein Stück Schokolade
25	**strange** [streɪndʒ]	*hier:* fremd

He looks at the chocolate again and he wants to take it, but he doesn't.

"Your mother is right. You mustn't take chocolate from strange people. But this isn't my chocolate," says the man.

"Oh! But why have you got it, then?"

"It's Rover's chocolate. I carry it for him. Can you take chocolate from a strange dog?"

"Oh, yes, I can take chocolate from a strange dog," says Ben. He looks at the old man and laughs, and takes the chocolate. "Thank you, Rover."

Then he tells the man about his adventure with the rabbit in the market.

"Where's your mother?" asks the old man.

"She's with my Dad," says Ben.

Suddenly the bus stops because there is an accident at the traffic lights. All the people in the bus look out of the window. A lorry with sheep on it wants to stop at the red lights, but it can't stop. It goes into a supermarket window and stops there. Now there are sheep everywhere.

All the people in the street catch the sheep for the lorry driver. A policeman has got a very big sheep, and he wants to carry it back to the lorry. But the sheep doesn't want to go back into the lorry. It doesn't look very happy and the policeman doesn't look very happy. Ben sees this and laughs.

3	**she is right**	sie hat Recht
15	**accident** ['æksɪdənt]	Unfall
17	**lorry** ['lɒrɪ]	Lastwagen
19	**everywhere** ['evrɪweə]	überall
23	**look**	*hier:* aussehen

"Look at the policeman," he says to the old man. The old man laughs too.

Three sheep are eating the apples at the supermarket door. The lorry driver can't stop them.

"Those sheep are hungry," says the old man to Ben.

"Yes, and look at those sheep over there next to the post office. They are eating that boy's ice cream," answers Ben.

"Do sheep like ice cream?" asks the man.

"Well, those sheep like ice cream," says Ben. "But look, now they are walking across the road. That's dangerous. The traffic lights are red."

10 **across** [ə'krɒs] über

He is worried about the sheep, but it's OK. The cars and buses wait until the sheep go back into the lorry. All the drivers help the lorry driver and soon all the sheep are in the lorry again. Ben's bus can go on now.

"The next stop is Long Street," says the old man. "That's my bus stop. Bye."

"Bye," says Ben.

The old man gets off with his dog.

2 **until** [-'-] bis
5 **next** [nekst] der, die, das nächste

Chapter 5: At the zoo

A few minutes later the woman with the big family of children says, "The next stop is Leeds Zoo, children. We get off here."

"Leeds Zoo," thinks Ben. "Hey, that's a good idea. I want to go to the zoo too."

He gets off the bus and follows the people into the zoo. The woman at the ticket window doesn't see him – he is so small. He walks into the zoo.

He walks around the zoo and looks at all the animals. At the monkey cages there are a lot of children. It is a children's birthday party.

"Here," says a man, "Here is a bag of monkey food. You can give the monkeys this."

Ben isn't with the party, but the man doesn't know that and he gives Ben a bag of peanuts.

"Thank you," says Ben. He looks at the peanuts and then he looks at the monkeys. "The sheep are hungry and the monkeys are hungry, but I'm hungry, too," he thinks. He sits down and starts to eat the peanuts.

"Hey, those peanuts are for the monkeys," says a little girl and sits down next to him.

"I know. But I'm hungry too," says Ben.

"Are the peanuts good?"

"Yes, they are very good. Here, take some," says Ben.

"No, it's OK. I've got a bag of peanuts, too," says the little girl.

9	**animal** ['ænɪml]	Tier
10	**cage** [keɪdʒ]	Käfig
12	**food** [fu:d]	Futter
15	**peanuts** ['pi:nʌts]	Erdnüsse

She starts to eat the peanuts, too.

Soon seven boys and girls are sitting next to Ben and eating peanuts.

A man with a camera takes a photo of them.

"You can see your photo in the newspaper on Monday," he says and laughs. "I think a good name for the photo is 'Eight little monkeys'!"

Ben wants to see the hippos now and says goodbye to the children. But first he comes to the elephants. He watches them for a long time. The zookeeper wants to wash them, but they don't want a wash today. They wash him and give all the people there a shower! Ben isn't wet because he is so small. He laughs when he sees all the wet people. He looks at the elephants again.

"The elephants are laughing, too," he thinks.

4	**photo** ['fəʊtəʊ]	Foto, Bild
9	**first**	*hier:* zuerst
11	**a wash** [wɒʃ]	eine Wäsche

Chapter 6: At the Pets' Corner

Ben walks on and comes to the Pets' Corner. Here there are a lot of baby animals and farm animals. You can go into the Pets' Corner and give the animals food and stroke them. The animals are not in cages. Ben thinks this is a good idea. He likes baby animals. He looks for baby tigers, but he can't see them.

"Where are the baby tigers?" he asks a zookeeper.

"The baby tigers are with their mothers in a cage," says the zookeeper.

"And the baby crocodiles?"

"Crocodiles and tigers are very dangerous. They bite. You can't play with them," answers the zookeeper. "You want to go home with all your fingers, don't you?" he asks.

"Oh, yes! There's a rabbit in the market and it bites. Look at my finger. Are rabbits dangerous?"

"Well, how many fingers have you got?" asks the zookeeper.

Ben starts, "One, two, three ..." He looks at the zookeeper. "I've got ten fingers," he says.

"Good, then rabbits aren't dangerous. But with a crocodile or a tiger, that's different. If they bite you, you don't go home with all ten fingers!" says the zookeeper.

1	**walk on**	weiterlaufen
3	**stroke** [strəʊk]	streicheln
5	**tiger** ['taɪgə]	Tiger
10	**crocodile** ['krɒkədaɪl]	Krokodil
21	**if**	wenn

"Now go and give the goats this bag of food. And remember, it's dangerous if you give zoo animals the wrong food. They can die. Every year a lot of animals die in zoos because people give them the wrong food. Some people give the animals plastic bags or toy cars, toy frogs or toy dogs to eat! Some animals eat these things and then they die. But your Mum knows that, I'm sure. Where is your Mum?" asks the zookeeper.

"She's with my Dad," says Ben.

The zookeeper wants to ask another question, but Ben takes the bag of food from him and goes to the goats. He starts to give them the food. First there is only one goat next to Ben; then there are four goats; and then suddenly all the goats, about twenty-five, are standing around Ben.

"Are you all hungry?" he says and laughs. "Sorry, I haven't got a lot of food. Look, now the bag is empty."

But the goats want to eat the bag.

"You can't eat the bag. That's dangerous," he tells them. Then the goats start to eat Ben's T-shirt.

"Now, that's silly. You can't eat my T-shirt. Go away!"

But the goats don't go away. Ben is a nice boy. He gives them food and he has got a nice T-shirt too.

"Help!" shouts Ben, and the zookeeper comes.

"Oh, dear, these goats love little boys," he says. "They think they're nice food!"

2	**wrong** [rɒŋ]	falsch
3	**die** [daɪ]	sterben
5	**plastic** ['plæstɪk]	Plastik
7	**I'm sure** [aɪm ʃʊə]	ich bin sicher
14	**stand** [stænd]	stehen
16	**empty** ['emtɪ]	leer

He runs after the goats and they run away fast. Now Ben can go to the baby pigs.

He watches the baby pigs for five minutes.

"Pigs aren't dirty," he thinks. "They are pink and funny."

The pigs run around and around. They don't sit down for a minute. One little pig is pink and black, and Ben thinks he is the boss. When he runs to the left all the pigs run to the left, and when he runs to the right all the pigs run to the right, and when he runs straight on all the pigs run straight on. But suddenly one pig sits down and then all the pigs sit down.

"The pigs are tired, too," Ben thinks. And he sits down next to the pigs.

He watches the animals and the people for five minutes, and then he looks for the hippos again.

1	**after**	nach
2	**pig** [pɪg]	Schwein
4	**pink** [pɪŋk]	rosa

Chapter 7: The hippos

Ben sees the lions first. They are sleeping on an island. There is water between the island and the people. The lions don't look hungry.

"They get food on Wednesdays and Saturdays this week: but they are hungry on Tuesdays and Fridays," says the zookeeper. "They eat their food and then they sleep and are very happy."

"Yes, they are very happy," says Ben. But lions are boring when they are sleeping. Ben walks to the next cage. Here are the hippos. Ben likes the hippos. But they look dangerous when they open their mouths. Hippos have got *very* big mouths.

"This hippo's name is Berta," says the zookeeper at the hippo cage. "Berta is fifteen years old. She eats three kilos of apples and twelve lettuces every day. Oh, yes, and she likes bread, too."

"Does she eat little boys?" asks Ben.

"No, she doesn't. She doesn't eat meat," says the zookeeper.

"That's good. The lions eat meat and the goats eat T-shirts and rabbits bite fingers," says Ben and he looks at his little finger. He wants to tell the zookeeper about Mr White's rabbit, but the zookeeper is very busy.

"What are you doing?" asks Ben.

"I'm washing Berta."

"Why are you washing her?"

18 **meat** [miːt] Fleisch
23 **busy** [ˈbɪzɪ] beschäftigt

"Because she's dirty."

"Does she like that?" asks Ben.

"Yes, she does."

"Do you wash her every day?"

"Yes, I do."

Ben always asks a lot of questions. He wants to know everything. Carol often says: *Ben is not a boy. He is a question mark.*

"Is the hippo a member of the horse family, or is it a member of the pig family because it has small eyes and small ears?" asks Ben.

"What do you think?" asks the zookeeper.

"Well, pigs and horses don't eat little boys," says Ben and laughs, "but pigs and horses aren't good swimmers. And Berta is. She's very good. Oh, another hippo!"

Another hippo comes up from under the water.

"Yes, that's Sammy. He often swims under the water for a long time. People say to me: '*Berta is lonely because she's alone here*', but I tell them: '*We have two hippos*'. People don't always see Sammy because he is under the water," says the zookeeper.

"Sammy is bigger than Berta," says Ben and looks at the two hippos.

"Yes, Sammy is a big boy. He's six years old, four metres long and he's very heavy – he's three thousand kilos."

8	**question mark** ['kwestʃən mɑːk]	Fragezeichen
9	**member** ['membə]	Mitglied
11	**ear** [ɪə]	Oh
16	**to come up** [kʌm ʌp]	*hier:* auftauchen
18	**lonely** ['ləʊnlɪ]	einsam
22	**bigger than** [bɪgə ðæn]	größer als
25	**heavy** [hevɪ]	schwer
25	**thousand** ['θaʊznd]	tausend

"Do you wash Sammy, too?" asks Ben.

"No, I don't. He doesn't like that. But he isn't dirty because he is often under the water."

Berta is clean now and the zookeeper goes away. Ben watches the hippos. Sometimes he doesn't know where Sammy is. Then he sees Sammy in the water on the left. Sammy swims under the water, and suddenly he's on the right. Then Ben can't see him again.

There's an apple in the water.

"Perhaps he's behind that apple," thinks Ben.

Sammy comes up again. He can't see the apple because he's got small eyes.

"That's a silly animal," says a big boy to his friend. "There's an apple in the water but the hippo doesn't eat it."

Ben looks at the two big boys next to him. Then he looks at Sammy again. Yes, the boy is right. Sammy doesn't eat the apple because he has got small eyes and can't see it. But then Sammy opens his mouth and it's *so* big!

"Wow! That hippo's got a big mouth," says the big boy.

"Hey, Tom," says his friend, "You're in the football team. Here's a football. Can you kick it into that hippo's mouth? It's very big."

"That's easy, Jim," says Tom.

"You can't kick the ball into the hippo's mouth!" says Ben.

He remembers the words of the zookeeper at the Pets' Corner: '*And remember, it's dangerous if you give zoo animals the wrong food. They can die. Every year a lot of*

22 **kick** kicken, schießen

animals die in zoos because people give them the wrong food. Some people give the animals plastic bags or toy cars, toy frogs or toy dogs to eat! Some animals eat these things and then they die.'

"Why not? I'm a good footballer," says Tom.

"No, no. It's dangerous!" says Ben.

"No, it's not. The hippo's in the water and I'm up here. It's not dangerous," answers Tom and laughs. He doesn't want to listen to Ben. He doesn't like little boys.

"That hippo looks hungry," says his friend Jim. "Go on, Tom, kick the ball."

"No! Sammy can die if he eats a football," says Ben.

"It's a little ball and your hippo friend's got a big mouth," says Tom.

5 **footballer** [fʊtbɔ:lə]   Fußballspieler

He kicks the ball into Sammy's mouth. Sammy doesn't look very happy, but the two big boys laugh.

"Look at its face!" says Tom and laughs again.

"Oh, no! That's terrible!" says Ben. "Sammy can die! He can't eat that!"

"Silly little boy," says Jim and goes to Ben. He picks him up and carries him to a tree.

"Sit up there, little boy," he says. "It's not a big tree. You can climb down later. Bye!"

4 **terrible** ['terɪbl] schrecklich
9 **climb down** [klaɪm daʊn] heruntersteigen

Chapter 8 : A hero

The boys run away, and Ben sits in the tree. He wants to cry but then he thinks of Sammy. He must help him! He climbs down, but he falls on his hands.

"Ow, my hands!" he says. His hands are bleeding but he's got no time. He must find a zookeeper. He runs and runs, but he can't see a zookeeper.

"What can I do? I must find a zookeeper," he thinks.

He asks people, "Can you see a zookeeper?"

A man says, "There's a zookeeper with the monkeys."

He runs to the monkeys, but there isn't a zookeeper there.

A woman says, "A zookeeper? There's one with the elephants."

Ben runs to the elephants, but there is no zookeeper there.

And then he sees a zookeeper with the crocodiles.

"Mr Zookeeper!" he shouts.

The zookeeper sees Ben but he's very busy, and crocodiles are very dangerous.

Ben must wait, but he can't wait. Sammy's got a ball in his mouth and that is dangerous.

Then Ben has a plan. He climbs into the crocodile cage.

"What are you doing?" the zookeeper shouts. "Crocodiles are DANGEROUS!" He runs to Ben and takes him outside.

Now Ben can tell the zookeeper about the boys, the football and Sammy, and they run back to the hippos.

The zookeeper goes into the hippo cage and takes the ball out of Sammy's mouth.

hero ['hɪərəʊ] Held
2 **cry** *hier:* weinen
4 **bleed** [bli:d] bluten

"Ben, you are a hero. If an animal eats a football it can die, you know, but Sammy's OK now," says the zookeeper. "But your hands! They're bleeding."

Ben looks at his hands and suddenly he wants his Mum. He starts to cry.

"Where are your parents?" asks the zookeeper.

But Ben can't talk because he's crying.

"Oh dear! What can I do?" thinks the zookeeper. "I work with dangerous animals every day, but that's not difficult. Little boys are different. I don't know many little boys."

An old woman sees the zookeeper with Ben. She can help them. She puts a jelly baby in Ben's mouth, and then she talks to him. He doesn't cry now and tells her his story. He tells her his name and address, too.

"Hey, that is a good trick with the jelly baby," says the zookeeper.

"Yes, it's a good trick. You see, you can't eat *and* cry. But now we must phone this little boy's parents," answers the old woman.

Ben doesn't know his phone number, but the zookeeper finds the number in the telephone book and phones Mr and Mrs Batts. Ben, the zookeeper and the old woman wait for them outside the zoo. The zookeeper talks to the old woman about the animals and Ben eats jelly babies.

"Ben!" says his mother when she arrives with Mr Batts and Carol at the zoo. "Oh, Ben! You're a bad boy. All alone in Leeds! " She is very angry and worried.

9 **difficult** ['dɪfɪkəlt]	schwierig
18 **phone**	telefonieren
25 **arrive** [ə'raɪv]	ankommen
26 **bad** [bæd]	böse, schlecht

"Ben!" says Carol. "I'm not going to town with you again. You're not old enough for the market. And then you go to the zoo alone! Linda and I want to have a nice time in town, but what must we do? We must look everywhere for you, and we are very worried. It's dangerous for a little boy alone in Leeds." Carol is angry with her brother.

The zookeeper stops her. "Your little brother is a hero!" he says, and tells Ben's family the story of Sammy.

"Can we go home now?" asks Ben. He's very tired. He wants to go to bed. But suddenly he remembers his Mum's cup.

"Carol! The cup!"

"What cup?" asks his mother.

Carol takes a cup out of her rucksack.

"Here, Ben, here's the cup," she says and gives him a cup. It is the same as his mother's old cup.

"Thanks, Carol." Ben gives the cup to his mother and tells her the story of the broken cup.

"Oh, Ben. I didn't like that cup." Ben's mother looks at his sad face and laughs. "But *now* this is my favourite cup. Thank you, Ben."

"Bye, Ben," says the zookeeper. "Do you want to come and see Berta and Sammy again? You can wash Berta with me and give them their food."

"Oh, yes, please," says Ben.

"Good, but the next time you must come with your parents," says the zookeeper.

"Now that's a very good idea," says Mr Batts. "No '*Ben alone in Leeds*' again!"

18 **broken** ['brəʊkən] zerbrochen
19 **I didn't like** ich mochte nicht
26 **the next time** das nächste Mal

Questions and activities

(Questions and activities marked with a ★ can be used as pre-reading activities.)

1. ★ Brothers and sisters

Ben is Carol's little brother. Have *you* got a little brother or a little sister? How old is he / she?

Does your little brother/sister get lost sometimes? Where? Does he / she go into town alone? Who goes with him / her?

Have you got a big brother or a big sister? Is he / she at school?

Do you like your brothers and sisters? Why / why not?

2. ★ Ben

Ben is four years old. Can he do these things?

Example: Can he play in a basketball team? *No, he can't.*
Can he eat an apple? *Yes, he can.*

a) Can he help in the kichen?

b) Can he play cards?

c) Can he read?

d) Can he play with a dog?

e) Can he buy a newspaper for his father?

3. ★ The story

Look at the *title.
What does the story tell you about? What do you think?
Does it tell you about

	Yes	*No*
a) a bank robbery?	☐	☐
b) the zoo in London?	☐	☐
c) Ben's adventures in Leeds?	☐	☐
d) Christmas with the Batts family?	☐	☐
e) an adventure in the park?	☐	☐

Now read the story and find out. Are you right?

4. Money, money, money

On page 8 Ben opens his piggy bank.
He has £2.20 in it and he can buy a cup with that.

£ £ £ £ £ £ £ £ £ £ £ £ £ £ £ £ £ £

You have £100.
What can you buy? *I can buy a ... .*

You have £10.
What can you buy? *I can ... .*

You have £2.20.
What can you buy? *I ... .*

title ['taɪtl] Titel

5. Partners

Here are two groups of words. Can you find the *pairs?

Example: piggy + bank = piggy bank

breakfast + ?
snack + ?
swimming + ?
birthday + ?
fish + ?
ice + ?
Kirkgate + ?
teddy + ?
pet + ?
guinea + ?
bus + ?
traffic + ?
bus + ?
jelly + ?
toy + ?

baby · Market · lights · stop · dog · pig · driver · time · stall · pool · cream · shop · bear · bar · party

6. Kirkgate Market

a) Make a picture of Kirkgate Market (in colour!). Hang all the pictures up in your classroom. Whose picture is best?

b) Play "shops"! One pupil stands behind a cheese stall; another pupil stands behind a bread stall; another pupil is behind a fish stall; another pupil is behind a toy stall etc. The class can buy cheese or bread or fish or toys etc.

pair Paar

You can say:

I would like ...
I want a ...
How much is that?
That is nice.
Please / thank you ... etc.

7. Who says what?

Here are some sentences from the story. Who says them?

Example: The kindergarten is never open on Saturday.
That's Mrs Batts.

CHAPTER 1
We're always hungry when we swim.
Don't worry, he's a big boy.
What do you talk about?
Look, here's my piggy bank.

CHAPTER 3
There's a cheese stall and there's a bread stall.
I want a dog for my birthday ...
This little brown rabbit is nice ...
Can you come and play with me again?

CHAPTER 4
A dog is a lot of work ...
Thank you, Rover.
Do sheep like ice cream?

CHAPTER 6
It's dangerous if you give zoo animals the wrong food.

CHAPTER 8
You see, you can't eat and cry.
Oh, Ben! You're a bad boy.

8. Animals

a) Ben likes animals. Do *you* have a pet?
I have a ...

b) Which animals do you like at the zoo?
I like ...

hippos goats crocodiles lions monkey elephants pigs

c) Make a nice poster for Leeds Zoo. Work with a friend.
Which animals do you want on it?
Hang all the posters up in the classroom.

9. Broken sentences

Find the two parts of the sentences. Write the correct sentences in your exercise book.

(1) Ben and Carol are …
(2 They wait for Linda …
(3) Ben looks for …
(4) He meets …
(5) She gives him …
(6) A rabbit bites …
(7) On the number 33 bus …
(8) They see an accident …
(9) Ben gets off the bus …
(10) He wants to see …
(11) He eats the monkeys' peanuts …
(12) At the Pets' Corner …
(13) A big boy kicks a football …
(14) Ben tells the zookeeper …

❀ ❀ ❀ ❀ ❀ ❀ ❀ ❀ ❀ ❀ ❀ ❀ ❀ ❀

… a roll and cheese.

… at the zoo.

… the hippos.

… about the bad boys.

… at the traffic lights.

… into Sammy's mouth.

… Carol and Linda.

… because he's hungry.

… a goat eats his T-shirt.

… a little girl with brown hair.

… Ben's finger.

… at Manny's fish stall.

… in Kirkgate Market.

… Ben talks to a man with a dog.